Living with No Balance …
and Loving It!

Living with No Balance ... and Loving It!

◆

A Simple Guide to Thriving in a Real World of Life and Work ... Even as a "Road Warrior"

Cindy Novotny

iUniverse, Inc.
New York Lincoln Shanghai

Living with No Balance ... and Loving It!
A Simple Guide to Thriving in a Real World of Life and Work ... Even as a "Road Warrior"

iUniverse books may be ordered through booksellers or by contacting:

iUniverse
2021 Pine Lake Road, Suite 100
Lincoln, NE 68512
www.iuniverse.com
1-800-Authors (1-800-288-4677)

Because of the dynamic nature of the Internet, any Web addresses or links contained in this book may have changed since publication and may no longer be valid.

The views expressed in this work are solely those of the author and do not necessarily reflect the views of the publisher, and the publisher hereby disclaims any responsibility for them.

ISBN: 978-0-595-47652-7 (pbk)
ISBN: 978-0-595-91915-4 (ebk)

Printed in the United States of America

Contents

When my book was first published I received many great calls, emails and notes from people who loved the message but wanted more stories. Lots has happened since then, so I have included additional stories throughout this edition in Great Moments as well in the content of my message.

Welcome to the next chapter … I have updated my book based on the last few years of travel and experiences. The new version will reflect some new thoughts, stories, and basically some great smiles.

This book is dedicated to everyone in my life that supports my ability to live without balance and thrive. My family has no boundaries and no barriers. My Husband Lefty has not only been the foundation of our dreams, but a wonderful business partner. His contributions on this book made it possible to complete. Jessica, my passionate and energetic Daughter, has embraced a life of living in a "non-traditional" world and on the road. She spends as much time in hotel rooms as she does her own bedroom. As Jessica has now entered the world of college, she is the first to admit that her life was "different" but she wouldn't change it for the world. Her entrance paper that she wrote for college was titled "My Ticket to The World." It was a snapshot of a girl who learned how to appreciate all walks of life without any barriers of communication or boundaries.

My Parents, Ed and Nancy, prepped me for this journey. They gave me the confidence to move every few years to a new city and adapt lovingly to the change. My Mother embraced "no balance" while making every house a home. My Dad has been the educational leader in our firm and is my constant mentor and coach. My sister Kelly and her family provide tons of laughter and fun. Too many people make excuses for not spending time with family and friends because of their busy schedules. This is no excuse for quality time. Learn how to make time not only on your terms but with terms that work for everyone.

Shelley Marlow, who has played such a key role in allowing our family to live with no balance. Shelley has embraced a lot in her life, and just this year has she has been diagnosed with breast cancer. We have all learned so much from her. How to have courage, strength and the ability to fight—all with the most positive attitude anyone would hope for. Thank you Shelley, for helping to keep it all together, with a smile on your face!

My creative and unflappable Media Director Bodie Lowe, who designed this book and put my words into print while excelling at his job at MCA concurrently. He continues to keep everyone laughing while making sure we don't take ourselves too seriously.

I couldn't do all that I do without my family or the energy and passion of the MCA team. Each member of the corporate team and the field trainers have embraced this lifestyle and continue to live without balance while loving it!

Foreword

Having a hectic life and travel schedule is something a lot of people are burdened with. Having a hectic schedule and enjoying it to the fullest no matter what are completely different issues. I wrote the original book during flights, layovers, delays, cancellations, and other "inconveniences" associated with traveling. I have been on countless flights and experienced all of these, but I always have a way to make it into the best situation possible for me. I now sit in a wonderful hotel in a great location—Singapore—working on some revisions to the second edition. Life doesn't get any better.

Writing this book started as an easy way to pass some time, then developed into an amazing recollection of experiences and tips I've gathered living a wonderful life with no balance required! Remember that you have total control of your destiny, if you put into it what you want to get out of it. Nothing comes easy, and by grabbing a hold of today will give you a life time of happiness.

Keep in mind that although I speak of no balance, my life is full of happiness, passion, family, friends and spirit. This is not about running on empty, but rather about living a full life! Since I first wrote this book, I have given numerous speeches and workshops on how to actually be happy without having to live with the "right" amount of balance. I can't tell you how many people have written me with great stories of how they gain back control of their life, by just enjoying the craziness. I believe balance is a choice—you have the ability to choose how you handle your schedule. So please enjoy the journey—life is a great ride and I would hate to have you miss the scenery.

Journey One:
What is balance anyway?

Or perhaps the more compelling question is "What is "balance" as it relates to one's life?" And who defines what balance is for any individual? Who qualifies to determine if someone else's life is in balance or not? I'm puzzled by how much **energy** people expend worrying about whether they are living a life in "balance" and trying to find happiness and fulfillment according to someone else's standards. In my experience as a trainer and leader I have found that those who call others' lives out-of-balance are generally envious because their lives are most likely boring and dull.

If you are really busy, you probably chose to be. You might work long hours while juggling multiple schedules and activities with your spouse, significant other, kids, parents, and friends. Your life probably includes everything ranging from social, athletic, and business events to more mandatory activities, such as renewing your driver's license, visiting the doctor, paying bills, volunteering, exercising, shopping … With all that—what is balance, according to you? Through trial and error over a number of years, I found out what "balance" means to me. This knowledge did what for me? It gave me a sense of purpose and acceptance of living "my way." You, too, can define balance for yourselves and enjoy life, as it is for you, not as it should be for others.

This book is written for everyone who wants to do more in a day than simply get the obligatory six to eight hours of sleep. It is dedicated to the working men and women who have struggled for so-called balance and have given up any hope of finding that balance.

Anyone who works, travels, enjoys life, has a family, or even just a dog will benefit from reading this book about living in today's world of too much to do in not enough **time.**

Webster's dictionary defines personal "balance" as "to bring into harmony or proportion." There is nothing wrong with this definition or concept except its limited nature—harmony and proportion mean different things to different people. And the problem we face today is that most people do not clearly define what those qualities mean to them or if being in harmony and proportion is really what they want. Instead, there is a tendency to get caught up in trying to live according to a general definition of the balanced, and therefore "good" life. But "good" and "balanced" are subjective states of being; thus, they inherently will mean different things to different people. Remember, you have a choice with balance. If you decide to turn off your Blackberry when you are home—so be it. But it you choose to keep your Blackberry on so you can quickly respond to a client or colleague because it will save you time tomorrow—your choice! Don't let anyone tell you how to handle your life at home or at work. It is your choice and never forget it.

If you are what the media and society refer to as a "workaholic" and spend less time with your family than you are "supposed" to, you might be branded as someone living a life out of balance. If you focus on spending more time with your family than work, but consequently might not be able to pay your bills, the contrary is true. You are probably perceived as being a balanced person. If you find yourself in the latter category, you might think society owes you for having put your family first and sacrificed additional, professional interests. But I ask, why not create your own personal brand of "balance" by living your life, exploring your interests to their fullest every day AND having it all?

Although society tends to treat workaholics—or those of us that live full, busy, fast-paced lives as professionals and family members—as social pariahs, I have fun being who I am. I want the same freedom from the stigma for you. Have fun being a workaholic, enjoy to the utmost whatever time you have with your family and call it a day. It's a good life. Some people are truly fulfilled in their jobs as they interact with others, express their creativity, and contribute ideas and solutions to their community, their country, their world.

For these individuals, and I obviously include myself among them, balance is fully participating in life on these levels. I see nothing wrong with that unless one **genuinely** runs themselves to the point of exhaustion and depletion because some other priority they have not yet identified goes unaddressed. But if that is not true for you, who cares what others think? It's your life and if balance for you is running around like a crazed person, I say more power to you! Due to my profession, I spend a lot of time with the younger generation of the workforce. These young professionals tend to want more balance in their lives until they begin to really think about their future. I am a personal coach to many young professionals who are searching for a mentor that will help them "have it all." Remember, it may seem "cool" to let your friends know that you are not going to "sell yourself to the corporate world," that you are out of the office at 5:00pm regardless of deadlines—until you miss budget and you no longer are employed. At the end of the day, everyone must produce results—it is simply your choice of how to produce those results.

Let's review another Webster definition of balance—"With the fate or outcome to be determined." Now that is an exciting definition. "In the balance" you do not know what is going to happen next or in conclusion. This is how I approach my life and it frees me up to be precisely whoever I choose to be and explore what I choose to explore. Instead of striving to incorporate society's generally accepted definition of balance (harmony, proportion) into your life, why not consider the excitement of what is "in the balance" for the rest of your life? By doing so, you will not need the balance of harmony or proportion, because you will gladly accept that you may never get it.

The sweetness of life in my opinion is about living fully in the uncertain moment, looking to the future, and **living** for what's in the balance. Webster also says that to balance is "to offset." You should offset what you do in your life by your own standards, ideals, likes, dislikes and what makes you personally happy and fulfilled.

When I first wrote this book, I was on a plane from Washington, D.C., to Miami reading an article in The Washington Post about the "stress of business travel" and how it is was destroying lives. I immediately drafted a letter to the editor with my argument on that subject. The people that write these articles generally don't travel like the "road warriors" they write about. What do they know about business travel stress and more importantly, what it is doing to the traveler? Guess what? In addition to being a "road warrior" myself and traveling 50 out of 52 weeks, I know a lot of other "road warriors" and life on the road is not that bad. Sure it is not as easy as it used to be. The delays are longer, the cancellations are more often, but the restaurants and shops at the airports are getting better by the day. So why is the glass always looked at as half empty?

Business travel is just one of many modes of living today that has been blamed for eroding lives. But it's just a scapegoat. Business travel is simply a thing that people choose to engage in—it does not destroy lives. People destroy their own lives by not living each day they create for themselves full of energy and enthusiasm. Take a look around at the long faces standing in line at the grocery stores, the arguments between family members at theme parks, the person on a park bench, frowning. Assuming that the conflict, drama, and appearance of dissatisfaction don't have anything to do with the periodic traumas that can occur in one's life, these examples reflect people waiting in vain for proportional balance.

The problem is these people will never find balance because they will never be happy with what they have. I was serious when I said business travel—and I'm not specifically talking about the cushy "business class" travel—is not that bad. Personally, I find that business travel has become less stressful since I accepted the fact that most trips will not happen without a problem and when I happen to say that aloud, I'm met with the disbelieving, judgmental frowns of my audience. How can someone scoff for expressing what is true for me? A real-life road warrior with a lifetime of experience racking up millions of miles and worn shoes living a life that satisfies me?

I recently gave a speech about this and one attendee walked up to me and suggested that I get in touch with reality. I look at the person and asked "what do you mean by reality?" Their answer was that they thought I had it made because I just spent my life flying from one speech to another. Are you kidding? That person has no idea of how much I juggle and manage—all with a positive attitude. Recently my husband and I went into partnership to open a new restaurant in our area—not just a small diner, but a full service, steakhouse and bar. We always wanted to be in the restaurant business due to the fact we love the world of hospitality and dining. You can not imagine how many people thought we were crazy. The comments and negative chatter about how you will never make money, people will steal from you and basically it will destroy you. Needless to say, that only made it more interesting for us. It has been open for years now, and success is what we are seeing.

So my story begins … all this fuss over balance, when the answer really lies with each of us. I hope this book will inspire you to take charge of your energy vs. your time and realize that balance is not necessarily the answer to **success.**

Your balance is what is important, by your own definition. Think of your life as in the balance … you do not know what is going to happen next or in conclusion, and that is reality and it is "okay!!" Think about it! Even the clichés try to convince us that balance is the answer … whenever things don't go our way we are told to "be calm." Even when life throws you a curve ball, "make lemonade out of the lemons you just received." So there begins the struggle … what if your life is a curve ball? What if you like lemonade? Trying to act like this is "a little bump in the road" doesn't work. The answer is accepting you can live with no balance while still "loving life." This is my story.…

I started my journey of living with no balance years ago growing up without a "hometown." No big deal. My father, like many others in the 1960's, was transferred for his job all the time. So my hometown was wherever we lived at the time, and where my parents called home. By the time I finished high school, I had moved eight times during my K-12 years. Although I have lived in Southern California for over 20 years, I have moved five times with my family of no boundaries and into a new home every three to five years. Some things do not change, and that can be a good pattern for you. Why believe that changing to a sedentary position would be better? I find it ironic that upon first meeting someone, the first question tends to be, "Where are you from?" When I don't immediately name a city, I get puzzled faces in return. Yet, I know many people who grew up in the same house, same city, and went to the same schools and still have no connection to the people they knew when they return to visit.

I have spoken to many people that have this same story and their lives are indeed messes. They use the excuse that they never had any real roots in their childhood—and therefore never experienced foundational balance—to justify why they now can't keep jobs, husbands or wives, or friends. I challenge these people to get real! The reason anyone has issues is not that they don't have balance, but that they are trying to live someone else's life. Don't make the same mistake. Live your life, create the type of balance—even the no-balance balance—and **enjoy** it while it lasts.

Loving life means hanging your hat where your heart is at that moment and loving it. For me, when I am not at home with my family (remember, I travel 50 out of 52 weeks a year), my home is a hotel, resort, or a conference center. Living in the moment and not worrying about what you think you should be doing differently allows you to enjoy the journey far more. How many people wish their lives away because they don't like their job, their living arrangements, their hobbies, etc.? Most of these people spend a lifetime searching for "balance." My suggestion is to read this book and find a new answer ... living without balance and finding happiness at the same time is possible. For the past 19 years I have spent literally every week on the road with the exception of short vacations ... all of which I still boarded a plane. Now please don't get me wrong. I travel all over the world and each trip is a vacation to me. I see each city and country I work in by taking a city tour or just walking around ...

more on my "monuments by midnight" later. Remember I am traveling with my colleagues, husband, daughter or even my parents or sister a lot of the time—and what could be better than that!

My story is about success and happiness, not about failures and sadness, and should give anyone who reads it a new look at their life as well as their journey. First, I think it is important to know a little about me, but not too much, because at the end of the day, this book is for YOU!

My roles in life include many … No Balance, No Boundaries.…

- Mother of a beautiful daughter
- Wife of over 27 years and counting
- A daughter and daughter-in-law
- A sister, sister-in-law, and an aunt
- A successful business entrepreneur and leader to my employees
- A restaurateur
- A farmer (we own a cattle farm in Iowa)
- A best friend
- A personal coach
- A very curious and energetic traveler

Like many of you, I live a lot of different lives, playing many roles. And though playing out the roles successfully requires a great amount of energy, I enjoy what I do. According to the generally held definition of balance I've been referring to, I do not live a typically balanced life. But according to my own inner compass and what I find meaningful, I live a personally imbalanced, balanced life. My hope is that by relaying my story and providing space to explore yours, I will arm you with the tools and ideas for how to live your own hectic, imbalanced lives passionately. I have divided the book into "Journey Notes" instead of chapters through which I hope will provide you a breath of fresh air, large doses of reality and some simple ideas for your **fulfillment.**

Throughout the book, I share a "Great Moment in Time" to offer positive perspectives on different situations I have encountered as I journeyed through life and across the globe. The "Great Moments" come directly from my personal journal and are meant to show you the "real" me living on the road, without balance and loving the ride. So, you've been forewarned—if you are looking for a book that justifies your misery about how busy you are, proceed no further and request a refund.

Journey One Notes:

Answer the following questions:

What is balance in my life?

Do I want balance in my life?

How many times do I wish for something different in my life? What do I wish for?

In a perfect world, what would my life look like?

Journey Two:
You are too busy. So What?
Get Over It

I have long admired the famous designer, author, and artist Mary Engelbreit** who coined the famous mantra "Snap out of it." Mary hit a nerve with this slogan/phrase with many people, especially women, and I believe it is time to resurrect it and add to it. "You're too busy. So What?! Snap Out of It!" And, even more appropriate—"Get Over It" And get over "Your Big Old Self." There is a fine line between "this is all about me" and "this is all about everyone else." Realize that everyone, and I mean everyone, in life today is busy. Haven't you noticed how fast time flies in this world of total and virtual real time. There is never time for anyone to take a break. The world will not allow it. So, don't just snap out of It, GET OVER IT! The ability to be connected at all times has caused serious frustration for some people. They feel there is no down time and therefore they are working 24/7. I have to disagree with this. I believe again that it is a choice for you to shut off your Blackberry or email and focus on whatever is important at that time. There are many times that I choose not to look at my Blackberry—at dinner, a show, visiting friends or relaxing in a spa. But I may choose to look at my Blackberry on the ride home so that I can handle things immediately and not have to deal with it tomorrow. It is a choice, not a demand.

Think about it. I have surveyed literally hundreds of people ages 5 to 94 and without exception everyone feels that time moves faster today than ever. Obviously time is still moving at the same pace, however our lives are consumed by so much and we are bombarded by so much that it truly seems like time must be moving faster than it used to. From kids to great grandparents, time is flying. Children email family members instead of calling, text messages have replaced the telephone and virtually everyone gets impatient when trying to download pictures from their vacation. No one feels like they have enough time in the day to do what they want. Now that is serious when 5 year olds and 94 year olds do not have enough time. What happens to the rest of us? Again, it's time to "GET OVER IT!"

** With a range of licensed products that stretches from cards and calendars to dinnerware and fabric, a successful retail store in her hometown, an award-winning magazine, more than 150 book titles published and hundreds of millions of greeting cards sold, the most apt description of artist Mary Engelbreit may be a line pulled from one of her well-known greeting card designs—she truly is "The Queen of Everything." Mary's unmistakable illustration style, imbued with spirited wit and nostalgic warmth, has won her fans the world over.

When did you wake up and decide that all the goals you set, all the big plans you made were too much and you needed a break? I believe the biggest problem in life is that too many people "dream" and plan their lives away, while taking no actions to make the dreams a **reality.** Compound that with the "lack" of time it becomes overwhelmingly frustrating and impossible to feel fulfilled.

Growing up, my sister and I learned some valuable lessons from our parents (I think all parents should spend more time with kids today teaching valuable lessons ... even from the road). My dad put himself through college selling copy machines for 3M, while my mom stayed home and raised two girls. She would help him write and type his term papers and, with very little sleep, still make time to read us stories, have a great attitude, and enjoy her life as it was at the time. No whining, no complaining about how her career was on the back burner—just living in the moment with very little money and very little balance. My parents set goals they both agreed were the priorities and they stuck to them: mom focused on taking care of my sister and me so my dad could complete his education. After the kids were in school full time, my mom set out on her career and became highly successful in the field of education. Today there is a difference: two people decide to spend their life together. They discuss their plans, decide on the type of house they want to live in, the car they want to drive, how to raise their kids (if they even want kids), and how to obtain the best job and begin their challenging careers. What's next is the pressure. They get the house, the cars, and the kids (or not) and the careers only become more demanding. At this point, people start to "cash out," either mentally or physically.

Why is it that society today cannot allow people to work hard and stay on course with their goals? I believe the answer is complacency, entitlement and good old-fashioned laziness, in addition to a constant search for "balance." My husband and I married over 25 years ago and set our goals. We decided that we wanted to work hard, give our careers a jumpstart, and then start a family. But the ultimate goal was to have our own company. We both knew that those lofty goals would take tons of hard work. Sure we had our "moments" where one of us would get tired, cranky, or just in the mood to take the easier way out, but we kept going. This **determination** is not unique to us.

There are millions of people just like us. And all of us determined souls sometimes could use a reality check before we let the imbalance of our busy lives tip the scales toward giving up. So let's look at the reality of overworked, unbalanced, and stressed out.

Who ever said it was going to be easy? There is not one success story in sports, medicine, science, art, business, music, education, law, or any other craft that does not include hard work, sacrifice, passion, pain, and the excitement of winning in the end. You might say it's easy to identify the stories of such people as Mother Teresa, Nelson Mandela, Jimmy Carter, etc., as success stories because these individuals made a difference in the lives of many.

But I believe all of us are famous, important people who make a difference every day. I believe that by traveling, speaking, and training thousands of people all over the world, I make a difference. I **believe** that giving my daughter a role model of a mother who likes hard work, challenge, and an exciting career makes a difference. I receive hundreds of letters from people who have heard me speak or have been in my training sessions that thank me for giving them the "kick" they needed to get back on track. That is a win for me, and that keeps me going—mile after mile. I also believe that having a marriage that works with distance pulling against it makes a difference. Too many people that travel blame the distance for the break up of their marriage. Not us. We have learned to live on the road successfully and keep a strong bond. This also applies to those of you who do not travel but work very hard in your careers so when you come home at night you may have to "work" at a relationship. We believe in living the life you chose and being happy with the choice. Sure there are days when you can easily think about a different path or giving up on your goals. But why would you ever give up on something that once meant so much to you?

What's the difference between these famous people and us? Those that scapegoat busyness for the problems in their lives expect wins to come quickly and easily. It's not that that doesn't ever happen, but when it does, it's the exception, not day-to-day reality. If you want to live for the exception, plunk down dollar after dollar for lottery tickets and … wait. But if you want to live powerfully, the first step toward your own satisfaction is enjoying, living, and loving life exactly as it is and extract all you can enjoy from each moment. Putting your energy into what "might be" vs. "what is" is my definition of "unbalanced."

Stop focusing so much on what you think your plans should be and start putting your plans into action by living in the moment. By planning, I am not talking about writing your life's mission, goals, and values. There are plenty of books on that subject that might or might not be of use to you. Instead, I am suggesting that you have a serious conversation with yourself, your partner, spouse, family, children, friends, dog, cat, or anyone with whom you share your life about what each of you want out of this journey.

Author Susan Scott devoted an entire book on having "Fierce Conversations" that force you to get real about who you are and what you want. It's time for you to take the same action. Too many people decide on the other person's journey, when in fact, at the end of the day, they wish the road took a different turn. Try it! Discuss how things are going. Be real, be honest, and as a team decide what you really want out of life now and in the future. Don't spend just a few minutes, rather block out an entire evening and focus. Who knows? If your neglect of these matters has created a possible explosive situation, the first exercise might nip the disaster at the initial spark. After the conversation, **commit** what you discussed in writing and you will see the amazing result of personal accountability. Please feel free to "Try it!"

Living with little to no proportional balance is not a bad thing. I said it earlier, just in case you missed it: Who said that "balance" was the "right" or "in" thing? What is balance anyway? Why do we all have to conform to some ridiculous definition of balance? Balance—having a great job that you don't spend too much time at (9-5), a perfect home life with a garden, fresh air, plenty of vacation and personal time, enough rest, but in the end—always behind the eight ball of debt, wanting more, compromising and simply accepting that you will never have everything you always wanted. I think that kind of balance is sad, unrealistic and not very smart.

"Great Moment in Time"

—London, England

I am at London's Heathrow Airport looking for some sugar-free chocolate to take with me to Oslo but I can't find any at the chocolate shops. When I ask a clerk for help, the clerk assures me that her security guard will go outside the airport and get me the sugar-free chocolate, which he does.

What is the big deal about this? An amazing customer service story and one more reason I love life. This is "balance" in my crazy world. This is why I love being in the moment. It is comparable to a champagne grape fallen off a vine; tiny but oh so flavorful if I take the time to notice. I could focus on being 5,000 miles from home and family or on the 12-hour flight I just took from Los Angeles to London, being tired and knowing I have a layover for yet another flight to Oslo, and feeling frustrated by not being able to find my chocolate. I could have easily fallen into a "pity pool" but why should I? Life is good and because I was where I was at the moment, I witnessed a small, simple, yet life-affirming event—some uniquely service-oriented "Brits" made my day—and my trip—the chocolate was fantastic! You also can turn imbalance into whatever works for you by simply noticing the gems of life that occur all the time.

An overwhelming majority of people I surveyed cited "lack of control" as one of the top reasons they feel stressed and overworked. When you search for proportional balance and continue to blame your hectic schedule for stressing you out, re-examine the pressure the word "balance" puts on you. Yes, use your discomfort and stress to indicate the need for more control over your life, workload, and personal time, but don't try to create more balance to get that control. No. That is a misguided use of your power. Instead, one way to gain more control is to eliminate from your daily routine things you don't like to do. Watch how the mind says, "But I can't afford to get rid of cleaning the house," "I have to mow the lawn," "If I don't do all these things, who will?" Let's think it through rationally because truly, if there is a will, there is a way.

What don't you like to do? Make a list right now. Forget whether you think you have to do the things you don't like doing. Simply make a list of what you want to get rid of now. Here is my sample list:

- Cleaning the house
- Cooking during the week
- Laundry
- Grocery shopping
- Gardening
- Sewing
- Feeding the Pet or going to the Vet

From this list, you might assume that I am not the domestic type. But you'd be wrong because I love doing a lot of things around my house ... just not those things. Here is what I love doing around my house:

- Decorating the entire home each month around a monthly theme
- Cooking on weekends
- Entertaining
- Organizing closets
- Painting
- Crafts
- Picking out flowers (just not planting them!)

So how do I do all the things I love and not the other things? One of the benefits of all my hard work is that I can pay someone to do the things I don't like to do. This is not impossible for any of you, regardless of how much or little money you make. It is possible when you prioritize to make it happen. Too many women and men spend countless hours doing chores around the house they hate and never have time to do what they like to do. Why? The answers are numerous, starting with the common excuse, "I have no money to hire someone to do this." The next question is, "what are you going to do about it?" Even if you don't work and absolutely cannot afford to outsource anything you don't like doing, create an exchange program with your friends. You will be amazed at how many people enjoy doing things you don't like to do.

There are thousands of books on dealing with stress, coping with anxiety, **managing** under pressure, and eliminating chaos through time management. However, there aren't many books that focus on making the changes necessary in your life to be happy thriving on the stress of life. What drains people's energy the most is working on things they don't like whether in their professional or personal lives. Consider seriously the things you do not like doing, figure out how much it would cost to have someone else do them, or explore who you could swap tasks with, and then create a plan to make that happen.

I have been using examples that apply to me; a married woman, mother, business owner, etc., but this opportunity for stress reduction also applies to tasks that men typically do. What don't you like to do?

- Mow the lawn
- Wash the car
- Repair things around the house
- Handle the finances

Whatever the activities are, figure out how to get someone else to do them. It's not that hard, but most people would rather complain about the tasks, rather than find a solution to make them happy.

We have identified that we are all busy. But what the exact toll on one's life is needs to be honestly clarified. I believe that the first step in this journey is to admit that you might exaggerate your stress, and have the ability to solve these issues yourself. No wonder it has been hard. Experts have bombarded us for so many years about the importance of finding balance in our lives. When I consider all the books I've read that preach simplicity, compromise, settling for average, finding what you love and then getting a job doing it, because then you will make as much money as you want, etc., it baffles me. How realistic are any of these strategies or goals?

First, simplicity ... I don't like simple (never have), so why do I read so many books telling me to un-clutter, clean out my closet, throw away clothes, etc? Second, finding what you love and then getting a job doing it, to make all the money you ever dreamed of, without hard work? Sure, it sounds nice to come home from an easy day at the office, be home by 5:30pm, have dinner on the table by 6:00pm, do homework with the kids, have a peaceful evening, and get everyone snuggled in their beds by 9:00pm. No stress = no reality! By now you should get the point. It is unrealistic to try to live your life in wonderful, no-stress balance, so why not enjoy the bumpy, high-flying journey and create the life you really want to live—without balance.

When my daughter was a newborn, my travel schedule was getting crazy so I took her everywhere with a nanny, and as Jessica grew, she still traveled with me one week out of every month. As a result, today she is a Premier Executive Traveler on United Airlines. But when she was in high school, the first thing I would hear from people is, "Well, you won't be able to pull her out as much now." Their tone is even a little punitive. Why is that? Sure, some teachers didn't like Jessica missing classes, but they couldn't argue with her straight A's and her great knowledge of the world. Is it better to learn World History in a Southern California classroom or to go to the heart of the Ottoman Empire in Vienna and see the history first hand? And when a high school history teacher has never visited some of the places he/she teaches about, you can imagine what my daughter brought to the classroom.

As far as the critics claiming my daughter has no balance in her life, Jessica experiences her life as perfectly balanced; it suits her preferences and she's an enthusiastic, **passionate** adventurer. In my opinion, the critics of her lifestyle or any-one's "out-of-balance" lifestyle reflect the human tendency to look down on others for doing what they themselves can't handle doing. Maybe you have those types of critics in your lives, too.

Here is part of the Entrance Paper my daughter wrote for college....

My Ticket to the World ... by Jessica Pierce Novotny

This small piece of paper I hold in my hand is the only direction I have left. Eager with anticipation, I sit with my ticket stub as the only proof of where I'm going. As high school is rapidly coming to an end, and college at Texas A&M University is approaching, I have only my dreams in tact. My life has been defined by hundreds of people and places, and I have the ticket stubs to prove it.

Hong Kong. 1:13 A.M. Flight 778 from Los Angeles International Airport. *I have just landed in a chaotic world* *much different than the world I'm use to back home in Orange County, California. The smell of perspiration pours into the air and the taste of raw fish swarms over my taste buds. This is my life, growing up on a Boeing 747 jet and traveling all over every continent. These travels have formed my existence, and made me a second home. I walk outside; my body is overwhelmed by heat and feels like I have just stepped into a sauna. The expressive lingo scatters around me, and my mind gets a little taste of their culture. This is a culture that I will always have inside me.*

Paris. Charles de Gaulle Airport. 8:13 P.M. Flight 819 from New York's LaGuardia. *Bonjour mademoiselle, tu va un taxi? Non monsieur, merci beaucoup. I have just arrived in France, the most intriguing country I have ever visited. I look out the window of the stretch limousine we're in and the city sparkles with flavor. I begin speaking French, forming an aura that I will take with me throughout college and on, making me an asset to whoever I meet along my way. Cigarette butts, bon-bon wrappers, and the lights reflecting on the wet streets from 'le tour Eiffel' are minute treasures that I lock in my brain and take with me on my next journey, the journey to the rest of my life. I start to ponder about my future travels. I reminisce about my past and only look at my ticket stubs for the future.*

London. Heathrow International Airport. 4:57 P.M. Flight 1125. *"Ladies and Gentlemen, we are now in our final descent into London's Heathrow Airport, please make sure that your tray tables and seatbacks are in their upper and locked position and we will be landing shortly." Those few words are like a gospel to me. From the moment I was brought into the world until now, I've heard that verse more times than I've heard a* *teacher say, "good morning class." I did not have the most normal upbringing and landing at Heathrow wasn't something I wasn't use to. Strolling down the gangway into the busy terminal, I glance out the window and see Big Ben in the distance, only a stone's throw away from the Tower of London. At the age of 12, when I took my fifth trek to England, I finally sat back and realized how much I have to offer the world with my knowledge and insights of the different cultures and places I've been. Not just traveling around the world, but grasping the views from millions of people has made me grow up very quickly.*

I'm on a voyage, a voyage no one else can take. Success and grasping onto it is not always an easy thing. My ticket stubs are a constant reminder of how I was brought up and raised and the many obscure places I have stepped foot in. It has molded Jessica Novotny and will finish me off being the Jessica Novotny with many memories, stories, and thoughts locked deep inside my soul. The moments of my decisions and where I go is the destiny that will forever shape me. The appreciation I now have for the people and the places I have met and visited runs through my veins everyday. I no longer look at any culture differently than I do my own. Whether it's the throwing of stinky fish in Pike's Market, Seattle or the hustle and bustle of the crowded streets in Singapore; I feel comfortable enough to call any place I have ever been my home. I'm me, and I will never be able to think any differently than the cultures and lifestyles I have encountered. Holding onto this stub today will and already has taught me to grow, change, and experience the world and what it has to bring to me. My parents set me on a path that gave me the courage, wisdom, and knowledge to look at the world as a small and safe haven. Others I know are scared to even leave their own town, but I now can do anything, be anything, and live anywhere that my ticket stub takes me.

These are my daughters' words, and will forever remind me that the **decisions** we made to live without balance were the best for all of us. Some people never take a risk and always wonder—what if?

I know couples who don't travel very often, and when either the husband or wife has a business trip, neither partner can figure out how to make it work. The couples become overwhelmed in the logistics. Who will take care of the kids? Who will watch the house? The pets? The plants? Oh my gosh! Get over it! Get real, get a life, and enjoy it. After all, those barriers sap one's energy to live on the edge without balance and provide too many people with yet another excuse to watch life pass them by.

This is the life we chose ... therefore we must accept it! Good and Bad! There are many times when the travel or work is like a dream and then there are times when you can't wait to get home to your own bed. Regardless of the situation, you can always find some good in each day.

By now you have probably asked yourself how I take care of the house, the dogs, etc. I made a decision long ago, I want the dogs, the garden, and the house, but I don't necessarily want to take care of those things. Don't you have friends that wouldn't mind checking on the house, maybe in exchange for something you can offer to do for them? Oh yeah, and your dog could use a vacation from you—believe me.

So now it is your turn. Use the space below and on the following blank page to write down all the things that you wish you could do, all the things you don't like doing, and what your plan is to change this. Commit this to writing and you will begin to experience how personal accountability leads to amazing actions and manifestations. Please feel free to "try it!"

Journey Two Notes:

What I wish I could do:

What I don't like doing:

My plan to change things now:

Journey Three:
Living on the Road and Loving It!

"Home is where the phone is."

I use this as my mantra since "home is where the heart is" doesn't work on the road unless you don't mind missing out on "heart." I can live anywhere as long as I can **communicate.** I know many people that live under the same roof with people and have a hard time exchanging 10 words!

Don't let business travel wear you down. Embrace it. Live it. Love it. Remember, you will be amazed at the results!

"Great Moment in Time"

—Las Vegas, NV

Here I am sitting in Las Vegas at the airport to catch a flight home—in enough time to actually have dinner with my family. I get to the airport in enough time, everything is going smoothly and what happens? There is a power outage at LAX that shuts down all air traffic control throughout the entire West Coast. I am going nowhere for at least six hours. Could I drive? Sure, if there were any rental cars left. Since I can't get a car, I have no choice but to hang out at the fabulously stunning Las Vegas Airport where people are going absolutely mad because there is nothing they can do about the outage. I, on the other hand, have learned to live well in the midst of expected and unexpected chaos-life with no balance—so the outage and the subsequent related problems are simply no big deal. I have the airlines work on booking the first flight I can take into Orange County or LAX and since it does not depart until midnight, I go ahead and make my plans for the evening. I make my way to a restaurant and order a Rib Eye and a glass of Cabernet and peruse my book of the day. Killing a few hours there, I am off to the shops (good news—Vegas is always open), try on as many clothes and shoes as possible, buy a few goodies to entertain me and then back to the gate to wait for the plane.

When I get back to the gate you can't imagine the depression on everyone's faces. They have all been sitting there for the past five hours, complaining to each other, calling home and complaining to everyone there, and literally making themselves and everyone around them miserable. Why? Their balance, their depended-on plan had come un-done. I never have or depend on proportional balance so nothing was missing in my life. Instead, I had a nice dinner and an evening of shopping. I hear people always talk about how they have no time for themselves to dine or shop. Not me! The rules might have changed, but not the **attitude.**

"Great Moment in Time"

—New York City

I am continually amazed at how the passion of New York City continues to embrace the passion of the people. Life on the road does not have to be boring, dull, exhausting, or overwhelming. How you experience life on the road or any type of business is all a matter of choice. And this time, I'm in NYC and it's a no-brainer how I want to experience the fabulous city's varied offerings. This time after training at a hotel and no family with me, I head to my guest room to catch up on work. Now, don't worry, I won't be in my guest room long. I spend about 90 minutes catching up with the office in California, emailing, and returning calls. Dinner is hardly ever in my room (unless of course I am on a deadline, want to watch a movie, or just relax). I find a quiet little café down the street from my hotel for my next "Moment in Time."

I walk into a café, which is jam-packed, and notice that there are a lot of singles at tables for two. Most people would never take the opportunity to ask the hostess if she knows if anyone that is dining alone would like to have company. But I ask. Sure enough there is a New York City Police Officer who is excited to have some company. We have a wonderful, great conversation and I leave having made a new friend. I find it so amazing that a lot of people would consider that too risky; like I was trying to "hit on someone." Why is it any different when you attend a trade show with thousands of people from all over the world and you set up breakfasts, lunches, and dinners with these strangers? I prospect all over the world for new business, new friends, and new ideas. And … It is great to have one of New York City's finest as a friend!

The first tip to traveling well is to make traveling a way of life and not a hassle. I leave my cosmetics and essentials in my suitcase all the time when I am home. The suitcase has its own little place in my closet, since it is not there long. I simply pull it out a few hours before leaving for the airport, pack the clothes, and I am off. I know people who travel a lot and yet when they return home they completely unpack their shower and cosmetic essentials, put them away, and in a week start moaning when they have to pack again. The key to success is to use the same suitcase no matter how long the trip. People laugh at my big suitcase. I can travel for a month with it, and yet when I go for two days, it goes with me. It is my traveling home. My briefcase, which is a roller bag, is a traveling office. I can work any time, anywhere, and be completely effective working on the floor of an airport while I wait for yet another delayed flight. These are the basics that need to be taken into consideration when you travel a lot:

- Extra batteries and chargers for everything—computers, phones, CD players, iPODS, etc.

- A travel pillow to use on the plane and more importantly on the chair waiting for the plane

- An iPOD and DVD's for entertainment

- Some cosmetics or shower essentials and a change of clothes should your luggage not make it

- Travel shawl or blanket

- All the reading material you never have a chance to read

- Most importantly, 'A Bite Before the Flight'—I'm never without food!

Now, what's **essential** for your travels or hectic lifestyle? What would make you feel better about staying busy rather than trying to eliminate the busyness?

So, what is the great hassle about traveling? It's what gets you where you're going—whether to an important meeting, gathering, journey, or home to be with loved ones. Plan for it, it's that simple. Of course, after 9/11 traveling began to test the patience of many. Snaking security lines at airports, threats throughout the airline industry, and lack of service are just a few of the issues that play on our nerves. But that's reality today. We won't change it by getting angry over it. We simply have to get over it. And doing so all boils down to a state of mind—the attitude you choose to have regarding travel.

What else is a hassle about traveling? When most people travel frequently, they are sure to be leaving family or friends behind, and this—according to experts—can cause a great deal of strain on relationships. Why does the distance have to create so much strain? Countless people come home every night to the same person, sit down at the same table for dinner, carry on the same "boring" conversation, and then wonder why their relationship is failing under that strain. Traveling as an issue alone does not strain a relationship. People who don't put the effort and energy into a relationship whether they are together or apart will never have a great relationship. If travel was the sole culprit of bad relationships, explain the high divorce rate in the United States—do all these people travel? I doubt it!

My family is the most important part of my life, and yet people would argue if that were true, I would not travel as much as I do. But none of these people will ever say that to my face. And yet, I hear my friends and acquaintances' accusations in comments such as *"When are you going to slow down?" "Don't you want more balance?" "You have such a lovely home, don't you miss it?"* My response to the accusations? Slow down? I won't slow down until I'm six feet under. Balance? Read the title of my book. Jessica has learned to live in a world of curiosity because of travel. I would never change what we did or how much we have traveled. There are so many of her friends that have had the great opportunity to travel with us, and all I ever hear from them is how lucky Jessica is!

So pay attention! Everyone who is looking to make a lot of money, work less, and never travel—get over it! It is not the reality of today's world, and yet you can still have an unbeatable marriage and be a fantastic parent. When critics in your lives tell you that you can't have it all, simply smile and say "I can have anything I want as long as I am **willing** to work for it without whining, face up to what needs to get done and simply do it."

Along with flexibility and making use of your time, another important aspect of living on the road is being able to conduct business on the road. Many people that travel act as though they can't handle the normal day-to-day operations like they would in their office. Why can't they? Let's take a look at a typical day on the road: 6:00am—Wake up and work out (there is a health club in most hotels or close nearby that are better than most at home). 7:00am—Get ready for work. Just like home, only you can have your breakfast delivered to your room if you so choose. 8:00am—5:00pm—Typical workday.

For me, the day includes training, speaking, and consulting with customers. Between appointments, one can check email, voice mail, follow up on calls, set professional and personal appointments, etc. 5:00pm—6:00pm—For those that didn't work out in the morning, now is your chance. If you don't need to work out, you can catch up on work, call the office (and depending on time zones, one reason I love traveling overseas; I'm through for the day and they are just getting started!). 6:00pm—? Now this is where the fun begins and if I were home there is NO way my evening schedule would look like this. Let me give you just a few examples of why living on the road is actually fun.

- Dinner with friends in different cities

- Movies

- Theatre

- Shopping

Monuments by Midnight—I learned this in Washington D.C. and now I tour all cities like this. I work all day, so I can see the historical sites at night by cab. They are really pretty with all the lights, and no admission fees!

Now could you do that at home? Get real! First you make dinner, do the dishes, rush out to a movie or go shopping, and drag yourself home exhausted and ready to start all over again. Some people might enjoy that, but we are not talking about how to love life at home in this chapter … we are **focusing** on loving life on the road. Milk the journey for all it's worth. Instead of getting on a 11:00am flight Sunday from Los Angeles to Washington, D.C., with a stack of work, buy a few magazines that you enjoy reading, a big Sunday newspaper, curl up in your seat and enjoy the most relaxing Sunday you have had in a long time.

Remember, at home the lawn is being mowed, laundry is being done, garbage needs to be taken to the curb, Sunday dinner needs to be made, but you are "relaxing." At this point for some of you guilt has just landed on your chest—"Oh great, now that I am feeling better about my five-hour flight, I feel so bad about leaving my spouse to do all the work." Move on—it's all about trade-offs. Remember, this is all a state of mind.

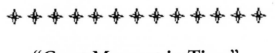

"Great Moment in Time"

—London (take two)

I was in London (again) recently for an entire week by myself working with several different clients and each night I was on my own. Many people, especially women, tell me that they would have room service every night, read, and watch television. Not me! And I suggest not you, either! I ask the front desk if they could book theatre tickets for "My Fair Lady." And they could. And when you travel alone, there are always great seats for one. So there I was … center seat, 10th row from the stage with several hundred of my "new" friends enjoying a fine musical. The next hurdle is intermission … everyone gets up with their friends and families for drinks and snacks. No problem, I simply go to the lounge, order my drink and before long, start chatting with those around me. Guess who was in the audience with me? Dozens of other business travelers (many Americans) that were taking advantage of London's culture creating their own balance! You don't ever have to be in a "lose" situation.

I have so many of these stories—dinner at a quaint café in Budapest, a boat ride in Prague, China Town in Singapore having some of my favorite local dishes, buying custom silk suits in Bangkok, walking miles in London during a tube strike, getting lost driving in Texas and the list just goes on and on. I have more energy and am less tired than most people I meet who are just going through the motions of "life."

Journey Three Notes:

Now what can you change in how you live your life that will **enhance** your enjoyment of it? Take some time and list those changes right now below. If you don't travel a lot, use this part of the journal to make changes in your work schedule. Commit this to writing and you will see the amazing manifestations that result from personal accountability. Please feel free to "Try it!"

What can I change right now to enjoy my work schedule or traveling more?

How can I get my family to "buy" into these changes?

What am I missing in life that I could begin to explore?

Journey Four:
Forget separating work and personal time ... Integrate It!

At the heart of work today is a real **desire** to find something you love doing and then get a job doing it. Meaningful work is creating the most value in business today. The talent wars of the early 21st Century have gone by the wayside and companies are back to looking for people that work hard and do not wallow in arrogance or entitlement. Even the new generations are learning how to work hard and still have a wonderful life. That is why so many young associates from law firms are found surfing at Huntington Beach, CA. in the early morning before leaving for the office.

At the beginning of the 21st Century organizations all over the world were vying for the best employees by offering all kinds of benefits: day care, fitness centers, casual dress, bringing pets to work, among many others. What was the result? People just kept asking for more and giving less. So now, these perks are gone and employers have begun to demand more from employees. It's too bad that we had to lose our perks, but we all wanted more out of life, more free time, more flexibility, more time with kids, and more money from the job. The key was more, without giving back to the job. One of the secrets to being happy is realizing that nothing in life is free. It never has been and all indications are that it never will be. So what does this mean for us? It is accepting that work is a part of your personal life. No longer can you really separate the two and be entirely happy with both your work and personal life. I have many discussions with people of all ages—Boomers, Gen X, Gen Y or whatever new term is being used today and I hear similar stories. Most people want to work hard, but they may work for a boss who clearly doesn't get it. Years ago I thought about setting up a website for people to report bad bosses—"Bust a Boss" was the name. Feedback from my attorney led me to put the project on hold, but I might have to resurrect the idea.

There are bosses who don't understand working parents; there are others who expect the young single people to put in extra time (because they don't have a family). Then there are the ones who expect "face time" versus results—it is no longer about more perks, it is about getting the job done, improving productivity, hitting the targets and still having a great personal life.

If you seek **happiness,** start looking at the cold hard truth, which is that although money can't buy you happiness, balance can't buy you a house. You can have both.... so make an appointment with your boss and ask how you are doing and what you can do differently to succeed at both. Make sure you are ready for the answer—you may not be working hard enough or producing results—if that is the case, make sure you are prepared to make changes in how you currently work.

I love when people say, "That's it! I'm taking charge of my life and taking off three years from work to sail around the world." Those same people end up running out of money, wrecking their boat on some deserted island in an unfriendly part of the world, and coming back to reality looking for "work." Whatever happened to taking a vacation? Work and leisure definitely go hand in hand. Why do people need to relax if they never work in the first place? Let's get real and stop avoiding reality. 'Dick and Jane' go to work and they come home and watch "Spot run." It may seem old fashioned, but it has been working for years.

"Great Moment in Time"

—Flying from Los Angeles to Kona, Hawaii

Everyone that works will relate to this story. Attitude is clearly my point of difference and I have talked about having a positive attitude throughout the entire book. It is important to recognize that while many people have such great attitudes, the focus seems to always be on the negative—problem employees.

Here is just another reason I love living in the moment and enjoying life in the present. On a recent flight to Hawaii for work, I was fortunate to get upgraded to first class which I love not just because of the seats, but so that I am more involved with the action—flight attendants, pilots and the conversations that go on throughout longer flights.

So here is how I got involved. About halfway across the Pacific, most people are sleeping, playing the "Halfway to Hawaii" game, or just getting restless. Not me, I am working my surroundings.

I hear three flight attendants talking about jewelry and looking at a huge assortment of necklaces, earrings, pins, and rings. I couldn't be more excited. I jump out of my seat and ask what is going on—one of the flight attendants sells custom made jewelry and she is sharing it with another flight attendant. Now the minute I ask about it, she gets nervous (probably the airline doesn't want her selling to the passengers) but I want to be sold to. I assure her that it is fine, and I end up spending a good 30 minutes browsing her 'jewelry store' high in the sky. I end up buying a great deal of jewelry from her, make her day and make mine even better! Now some of you may think again—how silly! There is nothing silly about it. I had fun, she had fun and instead of another airline horror story about a bad flight attendant—this is about happiness from both sides. She is living with 'no balance', too and having fun with it.

Work can be just as **exhilarating** and challenging as running a marathon, yet people get so excited for months in advance about running a marathon but on any given Monday they can barely drag themselves out of bed to go to "work."

I have found that if you stop separating the functions of work and pleasure you can enjoy the journey of both. The first step in this process is to make sure you absolutely love what you do. I know, you're probably thinking, "Right, how can you guarantee the job I get I will like?" The answer is quite simple. Did you apply for the job you are in? Were you accepted for the position? So what don't you like about it?

Here are some sample answers that I hear from people all over the world about why they don't like their jobs:

- It is boring

- I don't like my boss
- I don't like my co-workers
- I drive too far
- I work too many hours
- I hate my "cubie"
- I don't make enough money

The list could go on and on. So here are my thoughts:

- Maybe you are boring
- Maybe your boss doesn't like you
- Maybe your co-workers don't like you
- You don't read enough anyway, listen to tapes on the way to work
- If you didn't spend all day gossiping maybe you could get your work done and get home
- Your "cubie" is better than the alternative—being on the streets

Go ahead and look for a new job. Re-work your resume and head for the streets. After pounding the pavement looking for a new job, you will really know what your skills are worth. Good luck!

Although I might sound disciplinarian at this point, it's because I'm **passionate** about living well and it saddens me to see how many people get hired for jobs, become miserable right away, and spend the rest of their adult lives telling everyone how awful their jobs are. Just imagine your life full of energy and you are actually very happy. What does that image look like? Some time ago I was visiting a friend who married young, had two children right away, and held administrative jobs sporadically. She had a real desire to find a job with more meaning. We began to brainstorm what she liked to do in her "leisure" time and the answer boiled down to cooking and baking. There it was, right before my eyes—a catering company! At first she looked overwhelmed. Immediate thoughts of "I don't have a big enough kitchen, I don't have enough equipment," and many other possible barriers started to rear their ugly heads. It didn't take long for us to move past that and start to make her dream a reality. So there began a new country catering company called "Delish." (pronounced dee-lish) It all starts with a dream and doesn't have to end getting bogged down in the nightmare of what ifs, and I cants, and buts ...

My sister is another example of why you must **imagine** your life full of energy and happiness. She studied to become a dental assistant, went to work for some leading dentists in her city, and before long was facing what a lot of employees face—her boss was an inconsistent leader, people formed "cliques," and what presented the biggest challenge was the trouble she had managing her family and work. Her two boys were demanding a lot of her time (one son has a medical condition that requires her immediate attention when issues arise), her husband worked for the family business, and so the cycle began.

Wake up in the morning already tired, get the kids off to school, feed the animals (and I must say she has a zoo in her house), drive to work, and spend the rest of her day with her hands in strangers' mouths.

Please don't misunderstand me; there is absolutely nothing wrong with being a dental assistant, but the profession just didn't suit my sister. For her, the perfect job was working hard, but from home where she could control her schedule. So she began the journey to look for a job where her skills could be used while working from home. She found the right job and has never been happier. It took some time to find this new position working as an assistant to a successful entrepreneur in the sales industry and I guarantee she has more challenges in this job, but she now has the energy and time to overcome the barriers.

My guess is that most if not all of you have scoured through books about soul searching for what really fulfills you and how to turn that fulfilling activity into a job you'll love. The key to being successful in this endeavor requires more than just getting in touch with what inspires you but a strong dose of common sense. Do not fool yourself into believing that just because you love to sail you should get a job selling sailboats, or because you love to cook, you should buy a restaurant. Admit that any "job" you get will require you to **produce** results and create an edge. Without results, you won't keep the job you were so inspired to find. Just browse through the numerous bookstores out there or go online and look up "personal growth." There are thousands of self help books that talk to you about the secret of happiness.

Read them all—but I can assure you it all boils down to your attitude about life. It is not that hard to figure out. You get out of life what you put into it.… so enjoy the ride!

I would be remiss if I didn't discuss women in the workplace and why they are still struggling to break through the glass ceiling. What is happening to the bright, talented female executives in today's chaotic business world that keeps them from achieving the levels of success of their male counterparts? I believe the answer lies in their perpetual search for balance, which means they think they can't have it all.

Nothing is more disturbing to someone like me—a woman who accepts no limits to what she can achieve who thrives on no balance and does have it all. Most women in business today work as hard as their male counterparts, but truth be told, they don't compete as hard and haven't been able to deal with the "stress" of trying to find balance. Studies show that there is no difference in their ability to do the job, but what sets men and women apart in the corporate world today is simply how hard the women want to work. How sad! We are still being torn in too many directions and at the end of the day, never feeling quite fulfilled in any of our roles. Here, society and the critics of hectic lifestyles can really bulldoze women into feelings of inferiority, confusion, and plain exhaustion.

Over decades of working as a trainer, I've heard hundreds of stories about smart, educated women who after college "bust their humps" to make it to the top. What happens next is obvious—marriage, babies, and the struggle to find balance with being at the top. Why is it still the job of the woman to find that balance and why can't we **integrate** it all together?

Through several discussions with seatmates on planes, I came to know men who can relate to this conundrum, as well. Each man expressed a desire to lead a "sane life." Because of this trend, many men are leaving their fast-paced jobs in search of some balance between their personal and professional lives. What scares me is the withdrawal they have when the adrenaline rush of no balance is over, and, when they finally decide they have had enough "balance," they can't find a new job or return to the job they had left. In searching for balance, many women choose to "cash out," stay at home, and create a haven for their family, only to find out a year down the road that the haven has grown financial problems and the women is forced to "go look for a job."

I am not advocating as a "women's libber" here. On the contrary, what about the woman who has a great career, and when she has a baby, takes a few months off with the baby, and when the husband gets home from work, she immediately hands over the baby so she can relax and achieve some balance. Are you kidding me? The husband has been at work all day, commuted an hour to and from, is exhausted, and now has to work all night taking care of the baby. What do you do when you stay home with a new baby? Play, eat, and sleep! Here is another example of not living in reality. By my terms that is!

Journey Four Notes:

So what should you do? First of all begin by answering the following questions:

1. What do you really like to do?

2. If you could have any job in the world, what would it be?

3. What are you really "good" at?

4. If you were completely free of all obligations, what would you spend your time doing?

5. What type of "balance" are you looking for?

6. Remember Journey Two … what tasks do you want to get rid of?

7. How could you spend more time doing what you love and still make money at the same time?

8. How could you re-align your household, marriage, and child care to create more energy in your life?

9. How could you change your current job and make it more fun?

10. When was the last time you sat down with your manager and had a candid conversation about where you are in your job and where you are going?

Journey Five:
Create excitement for your life … Don't spend too much time planning for it

Everyone searches for happiness and many find it when they retire. Why wait that long? Creating excitement in your life can happen every morning when you wake up—regardless of "where" you wake up. I believe this wholeheartedly and have created excitement for myself everyday on the road. There's a quotation that I've loved for years: "Bloom where you are planted." Think about that quote. Whether you are continuously traveling for business or moving for your business every few years, or working to create a beautiful house and home for your family, creating excitement is easy when you focus on "reality."

Obviously, I travel quite a lot, so "home is where the heart is," for me, is "home is where the phone is." I can't possibly sit around idly waiting for things to slow down in order to **plan** for the future. I focus all of my energy on what I'll do today and tomorrow … Not yesterday. I believe today is all we have—so work it! I am fortunate that my family surrounds me on many of my trips, especially overseas. But I made sure that every employee on my team can bring their family along too. You can't imagine how much fun we have showing extended family around different cities. Husbands, wives, sisters, brothers, parents, children and even friends have also seen the world as we see it. Remember—this is the life we chose—therefore we must not only accept it, but embrace it!

"Great Moment in Time"

—Vancouver, B.C.

Today I am in Vancouver speaking to a large group for a few days. It is June, the weather is beautiful, and it is 5:00pm—Free Time! What a great place to be for a mini vacation—or is it?

I decide to walk around the city and take a water taxi to Granville Island for dinner. I get down to the dock and realize that I haven't exchanged any money since I was only going to be here for two days. The water taxi is cash only and it is $3.00 Canadian. Now this is simple, I can use American money ... no big deal, but I only have a $5.00 bill and the driver of the taxi has no change. Here is "excitement." I explain the situation to the water taxi driver. She says "Okay, here is what we can do. You can pay the round trip, but you will still have money left over, so where else would you like me to take you?" I don't have any idea of what is available, so she gives me a list of suggestions. She ends up taking me to a beautiful park where there is a jazz concert that evening. I end up getting a picnic dinner, glass of wine, and meeting more people than I would have just sitting in my hotel room. NEVER WAIT FOR EXCITEMENT ... GO FIND IT!

Some people might be thinking, "I would never go to a concert by myself." Why not? You go to the grocery store alone don't you? You will never find excitement by playing it safe. Sometimes you have to get out of your comfort zone to find more happiness. And since reality is that we spend so much time working, what a perfect opportunity to integrate our personal joy with our professional responsibilities.

Happiness is all around us (it is called life) and yet people make excuses everyday about why they are unhappy. I believe that a lot of trouble with kids these days is the unhappy homes they live in. They sit down at unhappy dinner tables, listen to parents who "hate" their jobs or each other, or worse. Face it. You chose this life, if it is not working you are the only one that can change it, but don't change it until you realize that truly things are not always greener on the other side of the fence. Changing places may not work. Try changing your outlook. I turned 40 years old sometime ago and had absolutely no problem with that birthday. To me it was just another great day of celebration—food, gifts, friends and fun. I love birthdays! Who said after you reach 12 years old you can't enjoy your birthday anymore? I guess someone must have said it, because that is why so many women and men go through a "mid-life" crisis. What is that all about, really? If 40 is considered mid-life, imagine how sad the next 40 years would be. Get over this once and for all. Who says you have to change jobs, spouses, houses or hairstyles just because you turned 40?

In this discussion of excitement, let's focus specifically on the job for a moment. I'm in sales—I'm a sales trainer to be specific. Unlike the majority of other sales-oriented people I know, I think prospecting for new business is exciting. It is reality TV at its finest. What other job could you have that allows you to talk to people (complete strangers) all the time for a reason? What other job lets you call these strangers on the phone day after day and make it a game to finally get them to call you back? It is exciting and fun to set your goals and to be worried sick if you are not close to making them. Take a minute and figure out some ways to make your life, job and relationships more exciting.

Planning for anything can be stressful, especially your life, but people get burned out for the most ridiculous reasons. Why are so many people teetering on the brink of a burnout? If you are feeling stressed, use this as a wake up call to reposition your life and create more excitement, shift your **perspective.** What you usually regard as a problem or a negative turnabout of events, start seeing as an opportunity to let your life hang in the balance of the unknown. That's exciting! Reviewing your goals and re-investing your energy in them will also help put things back into an exciting perspective.

I have spent a lot of time talking about becoming comfortable with imbalance. A big part of becoming comfortable starts with delegating responsibilities to others and NOT feeling guilty about asking others to take responsibility. After all, you might be creating some excitement in their lives by letting others do things and not hoarding the tasks all to yourself. How's that for perspective? Another tactic for increasing your comfort level with a hectic life is making things happen and not waiting for success with your career. It doesn't matter if you've graduated from college in a certain field and now you don't enjoy the work at all. Make a change and make it fast! It doesn't matter how young or old you are, seek out excitement because it won't seek you out!

It is time to live the journey if you aren't already doing so. In my opinion, we were put in this world to live, **thrive,** and enjoy each and every day! Although people reading this book are probably happy, there is usually room to increase our daily dose of happiness by dealing with reality as it is and not as we wish it to be, and living life to the fullest within reality's parameters. In talking about what changes would make people happier from every corner of the globe, some things that have come up are:

- Make more money
- Lose weight
- Become healthier
- Buy a house
- Have children
- Get married
- Get divorced
- Get a better job
- Go back to school
- Volunteer
- Take more vacations
- Spend more time with their family
- Get promoted

Journey Five Notes:

Now take a minute and write down the things that you would like to change or do to make you happier. Commit this to writing and you will see the amazing manifestations that result from taking personal accountability. Please feel free to "try it!"

Things you would change or do to make you happier:

So what do you do with that list? First step is to beware—excuses do always seem to pop up when people are trying to refocus their lives, change daily routines, or just simply work on making things better. Some examples of excuses range from:

- lack of time

- thinking it's too hard

- too many other obligations

- just not enough passion

The second step is to honestly take stock of what you are currently doing to achieve these goals. Consider the person who wants to buy a house or lose weight. They talk about their struggle, their strategies, their reasons for not getting what they want, but what they fail to talk about is their lack of implementation.

Clearly you understand by now how much I travel, and by no means am I alone in this. Millions of executives board planes every day all over the world to conduct business. Many people commute to their jobs for the entire week, stay in a hotel and return Friday evening to their families. More fathers stay home taking care of the kids while the mom goes out on the road and makes the money (read all about it in every "Working Mother" magazine). Among the hundreds of individuals I've interviewed, a majority feel frustrated in not having enough balance in such a fast-paced world. But for all the people who seemed to be whining for a different reality there were many others who refused to sacrifice what it takes to get where they want to go.

So go back to your list of what you would change to be happier. Is it more time with your family? More time for yourself? Make more money? What is it? The third step in achieving your dreams is to become willing to sacrifice to bring it all into your life. Who said that traditional "balance" is what it's all about? What is it about people that makes them feel they need a "schedule" that is the same, that they need to have "routines" that are the same, or they have to take time to "re-energize?" Most battery operated equipment actually breaks when it is not used enough. How about you?

In order to live your life without balance you must shift your personal paradigm. The late Thomas Kuhn, (Harvard affiliated scientist and philosopher) fathered, designed and popularized the concept of a "paradigm shift." A paradigm shift is a change in a way of thinking to another. Futurist Joel Barker defines paradigms as a set of rules and boundaries we all have. He took Kuhn's theory farther by **uncovering** amazing truths about paradigms and their effect on how they keep you from seeing your future.

- We have a tendency to use the past to predict the future ... and often that is not the best thing to do.

- Your past success guarantees you nothing when the rules change ... and they are changing every day,

- What got you to where you are will not necessarily take you into the future. It is time to change the paradigm you live in ... the way you think. If you don't, you will live a life of uncertainty—balance or not!

If you change your personal balance paradigm your life is limitless ... You too can live with no balance ... And love it!

While you are trying to find balance, re-focus, re-energize and "get a life," other people are actually living. Maybe if you stopped "thinking" so much about what you thought life should be, and actually enjoyed what it is you have, you would find the balance that I am talking about. Nothing is perfect, but you can make it close to perfect by deciding to live realistically and passionately in the world as it is.

When was the last time you created a mini vacation into your typical work day? When was the last time you had a major deadline due and decided to set at a park bench and complete your work? The problem is that each and every one of us has the ability to make our lives special everyday and there are no excuses to be miserable. Again, the questions are asked—"my boss would never let me go to a park to finish my work." "I would never just leave in the middle of the week and take a vacation day." Who said you have to take an entire day off? I am talking about buying yourself a better lunch, going out to breakfast before work, taking a walk at lunch, going online at lunch and buying a gift for someone. This is a mini vacation for me. I have learned to enjoy every day—even the tough ones that I don't wish to repeat.

I have mentioned before that I never have room service, and it is important to know I never miss a meal—Breakfast, Lunch and Dinner are truly my mini vacations—even in the heart of the Midwest where I grew up. I enjoy local dishes, talk to local people and learning more about life than university students who are writing their term paper on a certain culture. One of my trainers who has been with me for years takes pictures of every city she is in around the globe and has hundreds of albums to account for her great life. Another trainer sends her Mother and Father a postcard from every city—from sea to shining sea! These are just a few stories of how great life can be for anyone who wants to participate in it! Life is not given to you to just waste—it is given to you to enjoy and live!

Remember that any journey you take requires the energy and passion to complete the journey. I believe that passion is a combination of love and anger. If you really love what you are doing, it should royally "tick you off" not to get everything out of life you deserve. Maintain the passion by committing to the "Un-planned" and "Un-balanced" **life you deserve.**

Join me and other "road warriors" and anyone "living without balance", as we journey through a life without balance and enjoy every minute of the ride!!!

Always remember that you get out of life what you actually put into it. My Dad once said this to me and I carry this thought with me at all times:

"Don't despair about yesterday, or fear what might happen tomorrow, live today with joy and love in your heart and yesterday will be a cherished memory and every tomorrow will be full of hope!"

I am sitting in Bangkok, Thailand working on the revisions of this book. I have already been out in the streets among the hustle and bustle of this wonderful, enchanting city enjoying the smells and sites of Thailand. Shopping for silk, art and just enjoying the people has given me a mini vacation amongst a great deal of work. You don't have to travel half way around the world to enjoy your life. Simply sit back and learn to love the life you have—if you want to change it, than by all means take some action. The only request I have for you right now is to get out of your comfort zone and take a risk.... you will be amazed at the results.

"Final Great Moment in Time"

As I pull this all together I will share with you this final great moment ... for now.

I was rushing with my husband (Lefty) through an airport to catch a flight—what's new. He got in the line to check in just a moment ahead of me and I needed to move in front of a woman to get behind him. I excused myself and moved in behind my husband as the woman began to talk about how rude I was to her husband. Now I must share with you that I was shocked. It is not like I have never encountered rude people before, but it was unimaginable that after I excused myself to get in front of her, she still started ranting and raving about me.

Now, I never know who is watching—it could be the wife of the President of one of our largest clients, it could be a person who might be in my next session, who knows? The key is I can never let loose on anyone, but I am not going to ignore this. So I turn to the woman and look her straight in the eyes and ask her why she is mad at me. Now this was comical. She looked at me in disbelief and said "what do you mean?" I then mentioned that it was obvious she thought I took "cuts" since she was making no mistake about how mad she was at me—with that her husband looked at me and smiled—"oh don't worry about it, she is mad at the world!"

How sad—how can a person go through life and be mad at the world? You and I were all given a gift—it is our life. Take time to enjoy the good, the bad and ugly—that way you won't miss the **beautiful** part of living. Living with no balance has opened up so many opportunities and yet, I still wonder why so many people question why I don't slow down. Think about it one more time—if you have slowed down just because you don't like the pace—great! If you have slowed down because you don't like the pressure—find something new! Wherever life may take you—it is surely time to enjoy the ride!

Cindy Novotny is available for speeches, training workshops, personal and professional coaching. She can be reached directly at her firm:

Master Connection Associates (949) 589-6137

Or: www.masterconnection.com

978-0-595-47652-7
0-595-47652-X

Printed in the United States
207183BV00001B/197/P